Anna and Chen

Karen Vanderlaan

Chrysalis
BALM AND BLADE PUBLISHING

ISBN: 978-1-961261-01-3

Published by Chrysalis / Balm and Blade Publishing
1927 Mountain Road
Hamburg, PA 19526
www.balmandblade.com

Dedicated to my daughter Anna
and to the memory of Chenaniah (Chen)

Anna and Chen

Anna and Chen
are friends.

Anna loves Chen.

Chen loves Anna.

Anna takes care
of Chen.
She brushes him,

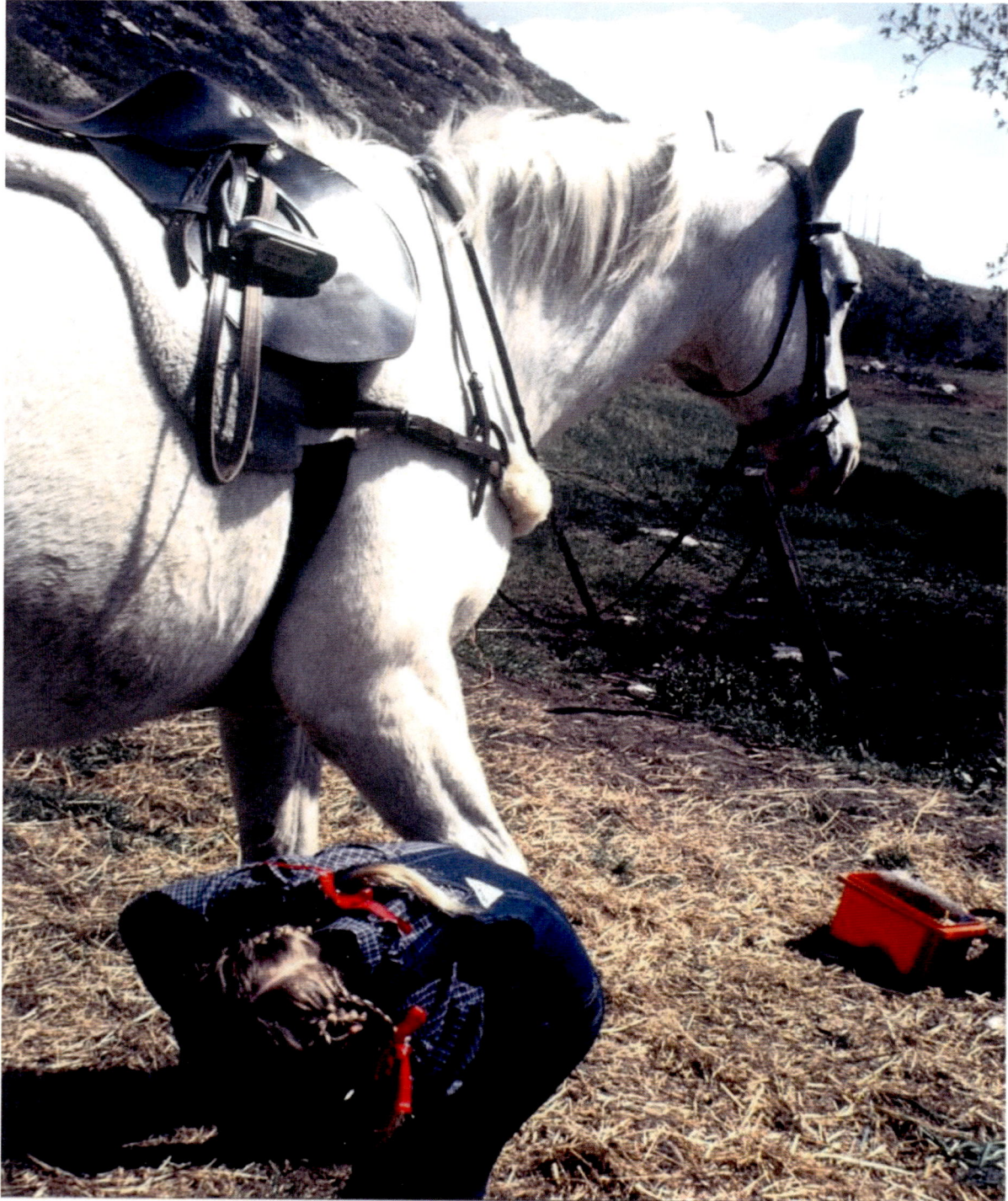

and cleans his feet.

Anna makes sure
Chen is warm.

Anna picks Chen's
favorite grass,

and brings it
home to him.

Chen takes care
of Anna too.

He never goes
too fast when
Anna rides him.

Chen is careful not
to step on Anna.

Chen listens to
Anna's secrets and
never tells anyone.

Chen never bites
when Anna feeds
him treats.

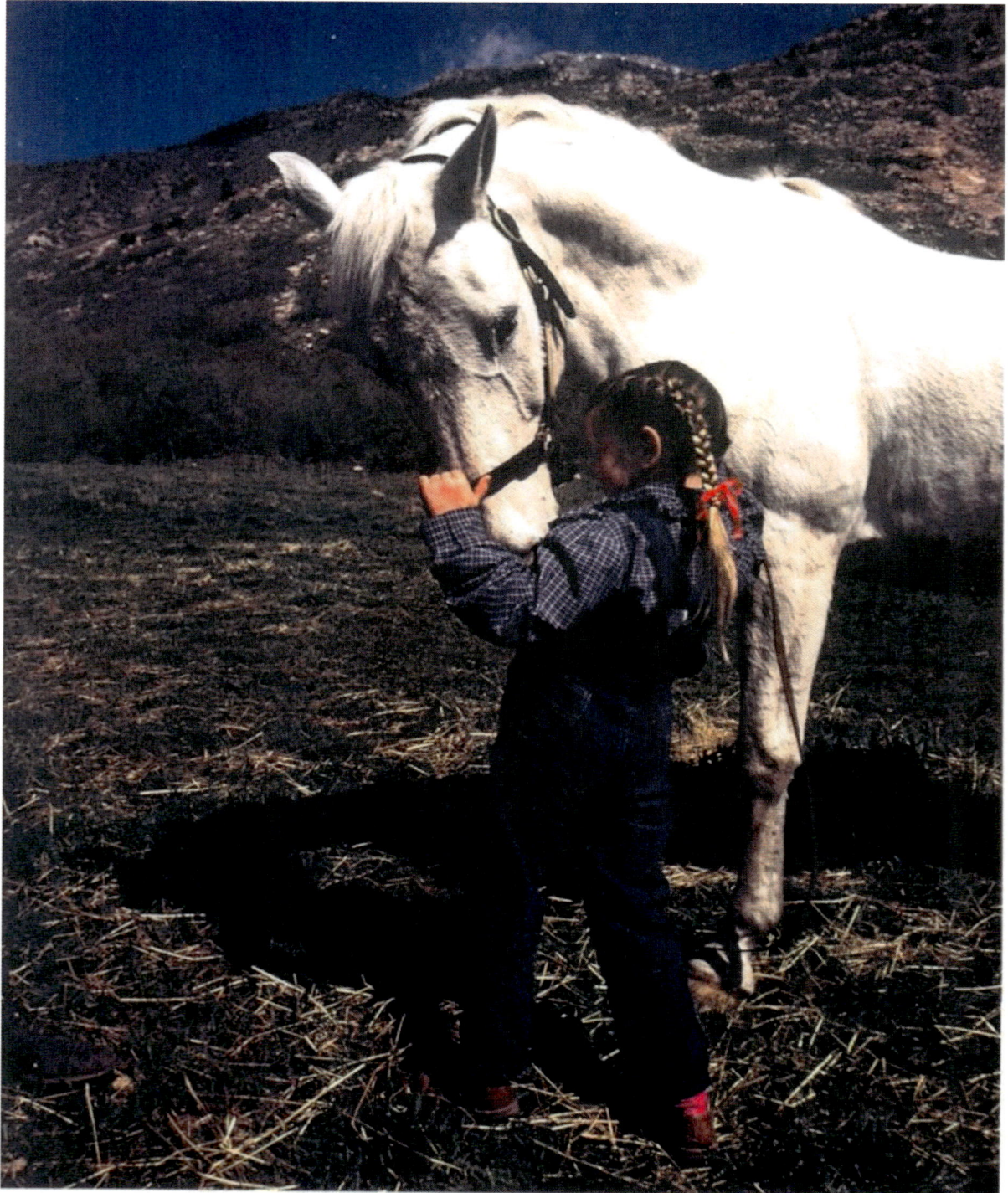

Chen puts his head
down so Anna can
give him hugs
and kisses.

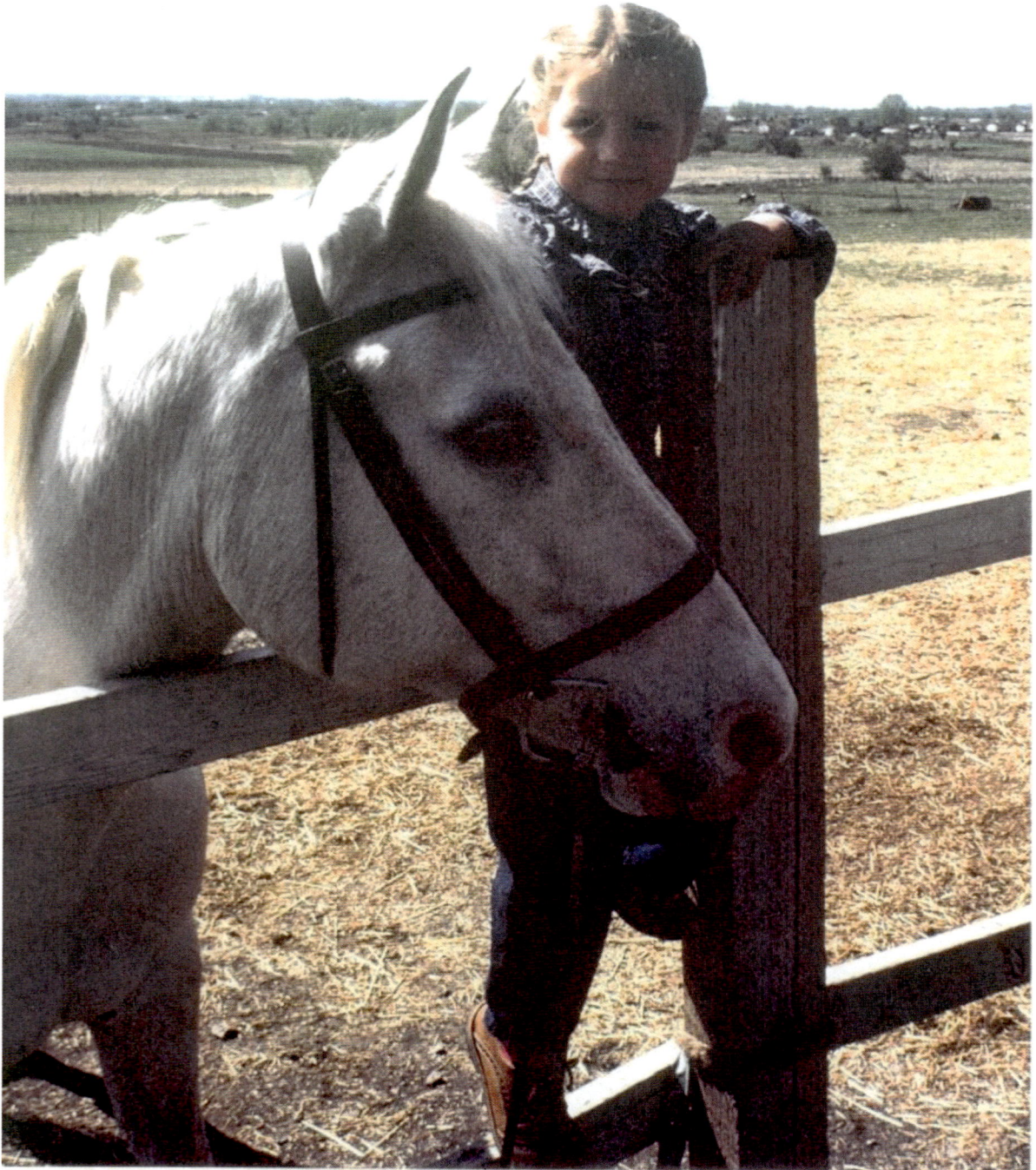

Chen loves Anna,
Anna loves Chen.

Also available from Karen Vanderlaan:

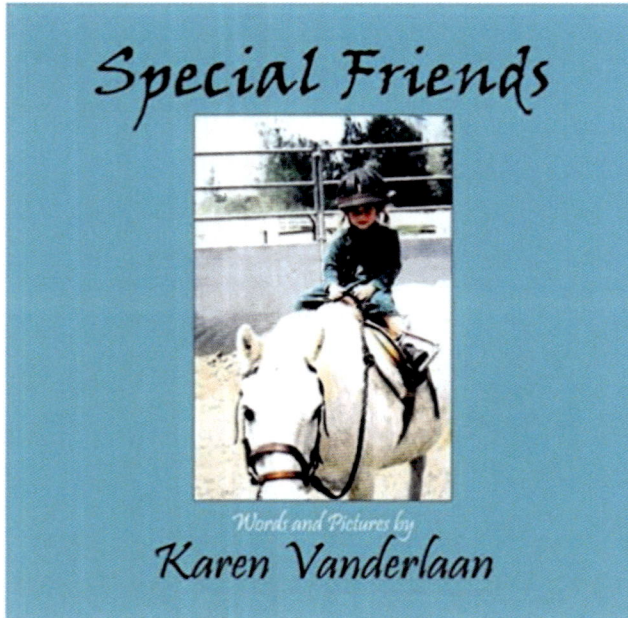

Special Friends is a tender story of a very young child living away from her home with her grandmother and a very old pony who was also sent away from her home. The two live on the same farm and form a very sweet bond. Crystal and Elyssa become the best of friends. The photographs are of the real-life Crystal and Elyssa.

Made in the USA
Las Vegas, NV
17 May 2023